and I feel as if I'm in the actual story! I hope you love these books as much as I do! – **Fiza Ali, Age 10**

I just wanted to thank you for these amazing books! I have 3 daughters, two of which are school age and they have recently been reading lots of Ninja Go books. We've been trying to find a better alternative for them to read and stumbled upon these, they are just wonderful! My girls are excited to read them, find them action filled and fun, while we don't need to worry about excessive violence or inappropriate language in the content. My life feels easier now thanks to these books, thank you SO much for your contribution to the Ummah, loving this series and we're looking forward to many books to come! – **Suzanne C., Mother of three**

My 8 year old has enjoyed these books immensely, she managed to finish each book in 2 days and has asked for more! We have made a small book club amongst our friends to swap and share the books, as mothers we love the strong role models the characters provide. We are looking forward to more books in the series!
– **Falak Pasha, Jannah Jewels Book Club**

A captivating series with a rhythmic quest. Some of the books in the series also have surprises that made me jump into the next book right away. It's hard to put down, but at the same time I don't want to finish the book I'm reading unless there's another one waiting for me. - **Misbah Rabbani**

We loved the Jannah Jewels books! There are very few Muslim books for kids that are entertaining. The Jannah Jewels books were very fun to read. They were so good that we read the entire series in two days! – **Zayd & Sofia Tayeb, age 10 & 7**

"I like reading books in a series, but the Jannah Jewels is especially great because I can look forward to a whole new place in history with every book. I also love the different personalities of the heroines, and my favourite is Iman because I love animals and riding horses too." – **Sarah Gamar, age 10**
I have a 9 year old boy and 5 year old girl. Both are very good readers now only because of Jannah Jewels. There are times when they were addicted to the screen. But Jannah Jewels changed everything upside down. The interesting characters, way of

narration, adventure, artwork and messages make it more real in my kids' world and help them take the morals to heart. It changed their behavior a lot and made them good kids. *– Shaniya Arafath, Mother of two*

My 8 year old loves this series - so much so that she has told all her friends about it, and one of them even gifted a couple more *Jannah Jewels* books for her birthday! In fact, I found myself reading her books much to the delight of my daughter - and then we both discussed our favorite parts. I love how the writers combine Islamic history with fun story lines and cute picture depictions. My daughter loves to sketch - and her books are filled with the *Jannah Jewels* character drawings. I would buy this series again and again. Thank you for all your wonderful work! *– Ruku Kazia, Mother of three*

Learning about Islamic history and famous Muslims of the past makes these books a historical book lover's wish, and the Islamic twist is a plus for young Muslim readers. *Jannah Jewels* has been Muslim Mommy approved as kid-friendly! *- Zakiyya Osman*

I love all of the *Jannah Jewels* books, and the fact that you combine history and adventure in your stories. I also liked that you put the holy verses of Qur'an that remind us to stay close to Allah and I liked the fact that in one book you mentioned the verse from Qur'an which mentions the benefit of being kind to your enemy. I have read all of the *Jannah Jewels* books and even read two of these books in one day, that's how much I like these books! *– Fatima Bint Saifurrehman, Age 8*

"We just can't thank you enough, Alhamdulillah! I just recently noticed all the characters in each book are actually real! MashaAllah, what a wonderful way to introduce them to Islamic history. I home educate my children and we are hoping to use each book as a syllabus for our world history now. Allah reward you for creating such an inspiration for our young today!" *– Umm Aasiyah*

It's important for girls and boys, Muslim and not, to have strong, non-stereotyped female role models. *Jannah jewels* bring that in a unique way with a twist on time-travel, fantasy, super heroes and factual Muslim history. It is beautifully written, engaging and an

JANNAH JEWELS

Created by N. Rafiq & R. Haleem
Written by S. Karim & N. Rafiq

Vancouver

To my Anse, my very own Sensei. - SK

To all of my beloved Teachers. -NR

Published by Gentle Breeze Books, Vancouver, B.C., Canada

Copyright 2015 by N. Rafiq
Front Cover Design by Jessica Dihiansan
Illustrations by Nayzak Al-Hilali

Visit us on the Web!
www.JannahJewels.com

ISBN:978-0-9867208-8-8

August 2015

Contents

Prologue 1

Reflections 6

Messages 11

Try, Try Again 19

Two Yeshuas 25

Breakfast of Champions 31

Fatima of Madrid 35

Giving Thanks 43

The Scientific Method 50

More Messages 56

Back in Time 65

Blinded 70

Sight 74

Click 79

HIDAYAH

Role
Guide
Problem Solver
Engineer

Superpower
Intense sight and
Spiritual insight

Carries
Ancient Map
Compass

Sport
Archery

Fear
Spiders

Special Gadget
Compass

IMAN

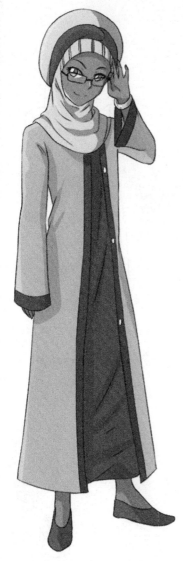

Role
Walking Encyclopedia
Horseback Rider
Poet

Superpower
Communicates with animals

Carries
Book of Knowledge
has a horse named "Spirit"

Sport
Horseback Riding

Fear
Heights

Special Gadget
Book of Knowledge

JAIDE

Role
Artist
Racer
Quran Memorizer

Superpower
Speed Racer

Carries
Quran
Sketchpad

Sport
Skateboarding

Fear
Hunger
(She's always hungry!)

Special Gadget
Time-Travel Watch

SARA

Role
Environmentalist
Marine Biologist

Superpower
Breathes under water
for a long time

Carries
Sunscreen
Water Canteen

Sport
Swimming

Fear
Drowning

Special Gadget
Metal Ball

JAFFAR

Role
Reader
Calligrapher
Painter

Superpower
Physical and
Mental Strength

Carries
Map
Bow and Arrow

Sport
Archery

Fear
Not Winning

Special Gadget
Personal
Time-Travel Machine

JASMIN

ABBAS IBN FIRNAS

THE JANNAH JEWELS ADVENTURE 5

CORDOBA, SPAIN

ARTIFACT 5: A VIAL OF SECRET SUBSTANCE

"Do the right thing by thanking those who have brought you to where you are. If you do so, you will be shown how to go forth in the right way."

~Scholar Fatima to Hidayah

Dear Reader, As-salaamu' alaykum,

Phew! What an adventure! For the first time ever, the Jannah Jewels were stuck back in time. How scary! But, Hidayah, Iman, Jaide and Sara proved once again that they could overcome their fear and work together to solve their mission!

They learned a difficult lesson about giving thanks to those who have helped them and that one of the secrets to happiness and ease is being kind and respectful to elders.

Up next, the Jannah Jewels are so proud to get closer to the half-way point of their adventures - but it is not an easy one. More riddles and surprising twists fill up the pages of this next quest.

Thank you for being a part of it all, dear Reader. We hope you soar through this book with delight.

May Peace be with you,
N. Rafiq

Prologue

Long ago, there was a famous archer who mastered the way of the Bow and Arrow. He was given the enormous task of protecting the world from evil. He was a peaceful archer, who knew an important secret that made him extremely powerful; not only in archery, but also in other ways you would not believe. The secret was written inside a scroll, placed in a box, and locked away inside a giant Golden Clock to be protected from the hands of evil.

But, the Master Archer was growing old and the time had come to pass on his duty to an apprentice. He watched his students carefully every day. The students trained extra hard to earn the Master Archer's approval. Two students caught the Master Archer's eye: Khan and Layla. Khan was fierce in his fights, made swift strategies and had strong hands. Layla was flawless in her aim, light on her feet and had intense vision. Khan wanted to be the next Master Archer more than anything in the world. Layla, on the other hand, just wanted peace in the world, no matter who became the next Master Archer. Finally, the day dawned when a new Master had to emerge. To everyone's surprise and for the first time in history, the duty was given to a girl—Layla. Layla trained relentlessly and over time, proved her just and peaceful nature. The Master Archer said, "It is only the humble, the peaceful and those who can control their anger that are allowed to possess the secrets of the Bow and Arrow."

Before long, Khan and Layla were married and practiced the way of the Bow and Arrow together. In time, they had two children: a boy named Jaffar and a girl named Jasmin.

Jaffar grew up to be a curious and gentle spirit who loved to practice calligraphy, read books, and sit for long hours under shaded trees. Jasmin on the other hand, liked to play sports, tumble in the grass, and copy her mother in archery. They all lived peacefully together in the old, walled city of Fez in Morocco, *or so it seemed.*

Khan fought with Jaffar, his son, every day, urging him to work harder at archery. Had it been up to Jaffar, he would simply have sat for hours reading his books and practicing calligraphy. He was just not interested in archery, but his father was so fierce that Jaffar had no choice but to practice with his sister, Jasmin, who was a natural. As the days went on, trouble brewed, and gloom and misery settled upon the villa's walls. Over time, Jaffar grew to be an outstanding archer, fierce and powerful, much like his father, despite his not wanting to do so. He soon forgot all about his reading and writing. On the other hand, Layla practiced archery differently. She practiced to refine her skills and herself; she never used archery for fighting, but for strength-building and purifying her heart. Soon, this difference in practicing the Bow and Arrow caused problems for everyone.

★　　　★　　　★　　　★　　　★

Far away in Vancouver, Canada, Hidayah was sitting in her classroom, bored as usual. She had always thought that nothing exciting ever happened, but today, everything was about to change. Hidayah was walking home from school when she spotted a mysterious woman in the neighbourhood park. The woman was wearing dark red, flowing robes, and something behind her sparkled in the sunlight. It looked as though she were moving into the empty house on the hill. No one had ever lived there for as long as Hidayah could remember.

Hidayah decided she was done with being bored. So, she started the long trek up to the house on the hill. She huffed up the porch stairs and tiptoed to look into one of the windows. She couldn't believe what she saw! It was the woman in long, dark red, flowing robes with a bow and arrow in her hands, standing so completely still that she looked like a wax statue. Her strong hands were wrapped around the bow, and her eyes were intently gazing at the target across the room. She was so focused and still that Hidayah had to hold her breath, afraid of making any sound. Hidayah sat mesmerized, waiting for the woman to let go of the arrow. *But she did not let go*.

So it happened like that day after day, Hidayah would hurry up the hill to watch this mysterious woman and every day, she came closer and closer to the door of the house. Several months went by in this way until one day, Hidayah finally mustered up enough courage to sit on the doorstep. Then for the first time, the woman let go of the arrow which landed in a perfect spot right in the center of the target. The woman turned and said, "So, you have come." She looked right into Hidayah's eyes as though she was looking through her.

Hidayah, at first startled, regained her calmness and with her head lowered said, "My name is Hidayah, may I be your student? Can you teach me the Bow and Arrow?"

The woman replied, "I accepted you as my student the very first day you peeked through the window."

Thus, Hidayah trained with the Master Archer for several years and was on her way to becoming a very strong, yet gentle, archer.

1

Reflections

S *tuck in Spain. We are really stuck in Spain!* The thought went round and round in Iman's head. Even though Hidayah had reassured her that it wasn't her fault, Iman felt very guilty. If only she hadn't jumped to the conclusion that the artifact must be ambergris. That belief had cost the Jewels so much time, and in the end, they didn't have enough time to process the next clue correctly.

When Jaffar told his sister the powder in the bottle was the color of Hidayah's scarf – it was a great revelation. But, instead of thinking it through to realize there's more than one type of powder that's red like Hidayah's scarf, Iman had again jumped to a conclusion - that the substance inside the bottle must be crimson powder, a well-known Andalusian product. Yet, after all that, the crimson had not clicked into place in the Golden Clock. It was all so confusing, yet the lesson to Iman was clear: *do not jump to conclusions!*

Iman tried to get the negative parts of her feelings under control. She didn't want to make Hidayah lose her resolve. Each one of the Jewels' good energies and positive attitudes were needed as much as their bodies needed food.

Iman took a deep breath and thought: "Now is the time to show strength and support! And trust in God's way of making things happen."

She quickly stole a sideways glance at Hidayah, checking on how she was doing. Hidayah's face gave away no clue as to her thoughts. The only feeling Hidayah gave off as she walked briskly ahead was *courage.*

It had been a long time since they had last eaten, but amazingly, even Jaide wasn't thinking of that right now!

The girls walked silently in a row through the Córdoban market. In the darkness of the night, the once-bustling walkways looked so different, the shops and stalls now boarded up. It would have been eerie if not for the warm, yellow streetlights that hung from the walls and lampposts.

All of a sudden, the Jannah Jewels were drawn out of their deep thoughts by the call of the Muezzin: "God is the Greatest! God is the Greatest!"

The words washed over them like a reviving breeze. They looked at one another and smiled. The call was a loving invitation to come back to peace. It made Iman think of a teaching Sensei had given: *You are never alone. As difficult as any situation might be, God in His Greatness is always still there.*

The Jannah Jewels made it to the Grand Mosque just in time to join the lines for the night prayer. As Hidayah prepared for this special meeting with God, she brought to mind Sensei's words: *The final part of the archery training is to keep a strong connection with God and His Messenger, peace and blessings be upon him, at all times.* Hidayah knew the five daily prayers were a big part of this connection. The Arabic name, "Salah," has many meanings and 'connection' is one of them – and this prayer was a connection for blessings.

As she raised her hands and repeated, "God is the Greatest," Hidayah felt she was transported to a different world. She wasn't in Ancient Spain, nor even in Vancouver. She forgot the artifact, she forgot her surroundings, she forgot the worries that had been on her mind. She felt she was wading into an ocean of peace.

When the prayer was concluded, Hidayah felt a tinge of sadness. She wished the prayer would go on forever.

As the other worshippers left for home, the Jannah Jewels stayed and continued making additional prayers. There was no rush to get anywhere now, no rush to beat the clock.

After half an hour of quiet invocations laced with heartfelt supplications for God's Help, the girls paused and took note of each other. It was then that Iman spoke out loud: "You know, I never had a moment to feel homesick on any of our missions

- we were always in such a rush. Now, I kind of feel homesick." A tear trickled down her cheek.

Hidayah lifted her hands in prayer: "O God, bring us safely back to those we love. Help us to get through this journey. O our Lord, Give us Your blessings in this mission. We don't have anyone to help us but You! Send us Your help – help that can never be beaten!"

The girls had no thought for where to go to spend the night. It seemed too far to walk to Abbas ibn Firnas' home. The mosque was safe and full of angels. It was so calm and peaceful that before they knew it, the girls had fallen asleep right there against the thick pillars and on the soft prayer rugs.

2

Messages

The light of dawn streamed across the sky and lit the rafters of the Grand Mosque. It was sunrise. The Jannah Jewels had awoken to the call for Fajr, the dawn prayer, and stayed awake praising God through worship. Hidayah remembered those early mornings back in Canada, up on the high hill, in Sensei's dojo. Every single morning, Sensei would sit still on her prayer mat, reciting verses from the Holy Qur'an and ask for forgiveness until the sun came up. She said that there were special blessings at this time of the day and staying up would help the girls to catch those beautiful blessings.

It was as if, with the dawning of the new day, the reality of their being stuck in Spain came back full force. It *hadn't* just been a dream, their being unable

11

to get home last night. It was true: this was indeed the Great Mosque of Córdoba where they sat, those were indeed orange trees outside, not maples.

Hidayah stared so hard into the carpet in front of her, she could have etched her thoughts into it. Worries tried to come back, tugging at her.

Why didn't Sensei show up in the tree? What are we doing wrong? What do we need to do to complete this mission correctly? Will I ever get the Jannah Jewels home?

Sara pulled out her metal ball from her backpack. *If there was ever a time that this could turn out to be useful, it's now,* she thought.

Jaide was waiting for a good time to bring up the fact that they hadn't eaten in a long, lonnnng time.

Hidayah called her friends to gather round her. She said quietly: "Remember how Sensei taught us: *turn your worries into prayers*? Before we face the day, let's turn all that we are worried about into a prayer, I'll start:

O Lord, thank You for this day,

thank You for the blessing of health,

thank You for faith

and for our Beloved Messenger Muhammad peace and blessings be upon him, the perfect Teacher.

Thank You for our Sensei.

Please be pleased with us,

and make Prophet Muhammad peace and blessings be upon him, pleased with us.

Thank You for all the gifts You have given us,

and helped us to unwrap to take the blessing of those gifts.

We are in trouble, O Lord. You see our problems!

You see our worries!

Help us!

Help us with Your unbeatable help, in this mission You have given us.

Show us the way.

Forgive us our mistakes, O You Who forgives even the worst and biggest mistakes.

Show us the way, show us the way, show us the way! With Your Love and Mercy."

Now Iman added her prayers to Hidayah's: "O our Lord, thank You for the knowledge You have given us, for guidance, and for good friends and sisters in faith. Show us what You would have us know and give us trust in Your Plan for us. Forgive us our many errors."

Sara followed: "O Lord, thank You for the beautiful sunlight of this morning, for the trees and birds, for the glory of this beautiful creation You have made for us. Make us walk upon Your earth with humility and in peace. You have given us a part in a great mission of peace for this world, and preventing evil. Please help us to play our role in the way that You want us to! Ease our every step and help us find the artifact."

Jaide finished: "O our Lord, thank You for all Your blessings upon us, for the gift of food to nourish us, for the gift of eyes to see and hands to draw, and ears to hear. Thank You and please don't withhold from us Your blessings due to our shortcomings. Show us the way. Bring the artifact to us in the most beautiful and easy way. And please, O Lord, bring us home safely to those we love."

Into the silence that fell after Jaide's last words, the girls together breathed, "*Ameeen*," and a peace fell upon them.

Hidayah opened her eyes. "Jewels, we need to complete the mission Sensei gave us. We can't let our worries hold us back and we can't let our own wishes to be home make us forget our mission."

Iman spoke up, "Jewels, I think we can do it. I know I was wrong twice about what was inside the bottle. But here's the thing: we know the bottle is from Yeshua's store, and then God gave us yet another clue. When Jaffar spoke to Jasmin, not knowing we were listening, and revealed that the powder inside was the color of Hidayah's scarf. We can all see, it's a red colour. Okay, so the powder's not crimson – we tried that. But, there could be other reddish powders at Yeshua's store. We just have to get over there."

Sara spoke up, "Yes, that's right."

Hidayah said quietly, "The only things I'm worried about are that Jaffar got there first or that even if we find it, we're still stuck because time has run out."

Jaide said out loud, "Jewels, all this is great and all, but I am sooo hungry, it's unreal."

Out of Sara's backpack came some dried fruit, dates, granola bars, and nuts. The girls shared them, and took long drinks from the huge water canteens in the mosque.

As they were finishing up, Jaide spoke up, "I wonder if Abbas is getting ready to make his flight today!"

No one seemed to hear her, and Hidayah spoke up again:

"Jewels, Iman is right. We didn't really follow Abbas's advice when he warned us not to jump to conclusions. We kind of did that a lot. Now, we need to do things right -"

She paused. When Hidayah said, "Do things right," she meant it to mean: follow the right steps in the scientific method, as Abbas had demonstrated for them. But after speaking, her words seem to echo right back at her, telling her a new message.

"Do things right" - it sounded like Sensei. Sensei had said they would receive messages during this mission, and asked them to pay attention to these messages. Hidayah felt guilty. She had been in such a rush during the mission, she hadn't paused much to hear the messages. Yet, when she had been in need, it was the words of the old man in the arrow store that had saved them. It was time, Hidayah decided, to start listening again.

Do things right.

Sara spoke up, "So let's approach this scientifically: we tried ambergris, and we got a new clue telling us that the powder is red, so ambergris is wrong. Knowing the powder is red, we tried crimson. But, crimson didn't fit into the clock, so we know that's wrong too. We know it's not ambergris, and not crimson, but it IS some kind of red coloured powder."

"What's left that's reddish?" asked Iman.

"I think we should go back to Abbas and get his help!" said Sara fervently.

"SubhanAllah, Jewels, I think Sara is onto something – " Hidayah said. Somehow, the words *do things right* were connected to Abbas ibn Firnas.

Hidayah felt so sure of this that she could almost grasp the messages slowly forming in front of her. Just a few more seconds and it would be clear enough for her to see it.

3

Try, Try Again

Before Hidayah could grasp the message fully, Iman sat up straight. "SubhanAllah! Look at this! Jewels! We've got something here."

The Jannah Jewels turned to Iman, who was peering at the ancient scroll that Sensei had given them, with the picture of the vial on it.

"What is it, Iman? I don't get it! What are you looking at?" asked Jaide.

"We need to get some water and a small sponge – there's another paper attached to this one. SubhanAllah, look at the way it is peeling ever so slightly at the corner here." said Iman.

Sara dug through her backpack and out came her water bottle, hair clips, tissue paper, candy, lip balm, a compass, a notebook, but no sponge. Sara balled up the tissue paper and dabbed water onto it. She squeezed out the excess water and handed the makeshift sponge to Iman.

Iman lay down on her tummy and began to dab at the paper. Slowly, she dabbed and peeled, dabbed and peeled. As she continued this process, the paper underneath the outer layer began to become detached. The Jannah Jewels sat, holding their breath.

Finally, Iman slowly, painstakingly, bit by bit, peeled back the entire top layer, being ever so gentle as to not rip the paper underneath.

The Jannah Jewels looked at each other wide-eyed and excited.

There, in the middle of the second paper scroll was another drawing of a vial with the same fancy stopper. Again, the image was not in colour, so they could not tell what the substance inside was.

"What does this mean?" said Iman.

"Wait," said Jaide. "There's something written here. It says: *If at first, you don't succeed, try, try again.*

And here – below the image, there is something else written: *Just as it may take two tries or more to accomplish a feat, it may take two artifacts or more a mission to complete!*"

"Wow!" said Jaide.

"Oh SubhanAllah! So wait, this means…there are two bottles to collect?!"

"I bet you need *both* of the vials in the Golden Clock, one at 4 o'clock and one at 5 o'clock!" said Sara. "Kind of like, this is our fifth mission!"

Sara said, "Sensei was right about the blessings of staying up til sunrise. We stayed up for sunrise and God rewarded us with the blessing of figuring out this super important part of our mission!"

Jaide said, "OK, this is getting confusing. I need to write this all down." She pulled out her sketchpad and wrote down the clues they had:

CLUE	SOURCE
We need two bottles	the Scrolls from Sensei
The bottles are both from Yeshua's store	Abbas ibn Firnas, who told us they have Yeshua's signature stopper

The artifact (bottle contents) should be something important to the time, place or people we are visiting	Abbas helped us figure this out
Contents of at least one bottle are red	Jaffar
Contents are *not* crimson	Did not fit into clock

"Does that sound right, girls?"

"Yes."

Iman spoke, "So...girls...this means...we need to forget about the crimson, and find two more bottles, from Yeshua's store, one with a red powder, as Jaffar was looking for...and one other one, not necessarily red. I mean, it could STILL be ambergris, after all."

"I sure hope it's NOT ambergris. You know who has the only ambergris in that kind of bottle – Jasmin! I don't want to fight her again!" exclaimed Jaide.

"Well, we don't know. It could be ambergris, or something else. How about we focus on getting to Yehsua's store first!"

"But girls, don't you think we should go and ask Abbas first?" asked Sara, quietly.

Iman spoke, "We don't have time. We need to get to Yeshua's – we need to get there before he leaves on his trip today for the Holy Land!"

4

Two Yeshuas

With no time to lose, the girls took their quickest means of transport. Iman whistled for her horse, Spirit, and she and Hidayah jumped on; Sarah and Jaide climbed on Jaide's skateboard. Before they knew it, they were in the square where Yeshua ben Yousef's store was located. The morning was fresh and clear.

Merchants in the square were just opening up their front doors. The air was filled with the scent of orange blossoms. Hidayah loved this time of day, it was so full of hope for good things to come.

They ran towards Yeshua's store. Suddenly, they stopped. Jaide let out a low cry. Something was wrong.

Yeshua ben Yousef's store had been transformed: no longer was it shrouded with mystery, dimly lit and stocked with potions all along its shelves – instead, it looked very much like a modern pharmacy.

Hidayah turned to look at Sara, Iman and Jaide as they all stood at the threshold of the store.

"Is this the place, girls?" asked Hidayah.

"Yes, it is Hidayah. This is where it was last night," Iman assured her.

Not knowing what else to do, Hidayah breathed deeply.

"Bismillahir-Rahmanir-Rahim."

"Is... is... Yeshua ben Yosef here?" Hidayah asked hesitantly.

"I am Yeshua ben Yosef. How can I help you?" said a young man with a smooth beard and twinkly eyes. He was wearing a long, white coat that reached down to his knees, stiff and clean with broad collars, it had a small pocket on the left side of his chest with a quill-like pen inside it. Just like a pharmacist at any store back in Vancouver. There, just above the small pocket was his name embroidered in black thread – Yeshua ben Yousef. But it wasn't Yeshua at all!

"*You* are Yeshua?" asked Jaide. "You are certainly not!"

The man who stood before them looked a little taken aback.

"I am not sure how to answer that…but let me try to be professional here. How can I help you?"

Iman spoke up: "Well… we need something from this store… we need some…you know, powders and things."

"Do you have a prescription?" he said.

"Prescription?!" said Iman.

"I'm sorry Miss. These are the Prince's orders. No issuing of any substances without a prescription from a registered doctor," and he pointed at a framed letter on the wall.

The girls peered closer at the letter. It stated exactly what Yeshua had just said, and was signed, "Al Hakam III."

Inside the glass cabinets behind the pharmacist were all kinds of bottles, but none with the distinctive stopper they were looking for.

Hidayah narrowed her eyes and addressed the pharmacist one more time, "You sure you're Mr. Yeshua? You're not just replacing him while he's visiting the Holy Land?"

The young man laughed, "Yes miss, I'm sure. I'm the owner of this premises – I'm not replacing anyone. But I sure would like to visit the Holy Land one day!"

The girls slowly turned around, heading back towards the door and out into the sunshine.

They stopped in a corner of the square, and all sat down at the foot of a tree.

"Ummm…something's going on here…" started Sara.

Jaide took out her sketchbook. She turned through the pages, looking up from them to the square before her, and then back to them. "Girls, something major has changed, *overnight*."

"There was something I wanted to tell you girls this morning. In the Grand Mosque's courtyard, I noticed that the trees looked different. They are bigger than before," said Sara. Sara had a powerful awareness of her environment. She cared for it so deeply that it was always the first thing she noticed.

"What's happened? Where are we? Are we in a different place?" asked Hidayah, bewildered.

"We're still in Spain...but I think the real question is," said Iman, "WHEN are we?"

"*When* are we? What, have we travelled in time again?" asked Hidayah, incredulously.

Jaide looked down at her watch. "Look!" she held out her wrist. "My watch has stopped- and it's at a different time than it was when I last looked at it. When I last looked at it, as we ran for the tree, it was at 0:00. Now, it's at 1:00 and – and - it's not moving!"

The square was certainly different than when they had last seen it. There were many more dentists and doctor's offices. The girls' eyes scanned the lines of shops on all four sides, looking for the stores they had visited only the day before.

"The archery supply store is gone!" said Jaide.

"Oh God!" breathed Hidayah.

5

Breakfast of Champions

After what seemed like an endless silence, Jaide spoke up: "Jewels, what hasn't changed is one thing I know for sure: I'm super hungry. We haven't eaten a proper meal in...ages!"

"Yes. Approximately 200 years," said Iman, looking up from the Book of Knowledge. "According to my calculations, based on the fact that the ruler right now is Al Hakam III, and confirmed by our observations - we are in Andalusia, circa the year... 1000!"

"What?!" said Jaide. "We've moved ahead in time?? But we are still in Ancient Spain?"

"Yes," said Iman.

"I just hope we aren't closer to any disasters. I don't want to get caught up in the middle of a mess," said Jaide.

"Don't worry," said Iman. "Things are still going to be okay round here for approximately another 492 years."

"Phe-yewwww," said Jaide.

Hidayah was not able to focus. It had just hit her: they would not be able to leave downtown to find the home that they had once been welcomed into. Their friend, Abbas ibn Firnas...was a man of the past. Where were they going to go now? Who would offer them the guidance they needed? Who could help them understand how to "do things right"?

Hidayah reminded herself that there had to be a reason why all this was happening. She reminded herself to listen for the messages, and not lose hope in God. She resolved to stay positive. "God does all things for a reason. God, we rely on You completely. You would never let us down," said Hidayah, out loud. Her friends smiled. They were relieved that Hidayah had gotten the bounce back in her step.

"Something will come up to show us the way, girls. Our test right now is to not freak out. Okay, so we need bottles from Yeshua's store, and it doesn't even exist anymore. Plus, we are stuck in Spain, but God is Merciful, and has the Power to help us."

"That's right!" said Jaide. "There's no point getting stressed out. Let's just relax and let God carry us through this."

"Blessed, not stressed!" added Jaide with a big smile.

The girls made their way back through the market, which was now filling up with crowds. Even the look of the people in the crowds were somewhat different. The clothes they wore seemed to be wrapped and decorated in a different style than what the Jannah Jewels had seen in town just the day before.

The girls stopped at a stall in the market that was selling something like churros. They were sweet pastries sprinkled with sugar and orange blossom water. Jaide was overjoyed: "Mmm....this makes up for being lost in time!" she declared with a wink at her friends.

They rolled their eyes but smiled in spite of themselves. It was such a blessing to have something warm and sweet to eat.

The girls stood around near the stall ordering seconds. Suddenly, they found their feet being carried forward. "Hey!" yelled Jaide. They had been swept up in a crowd that was moving in a wave through the thin winding streets of the marketplace. They found themselves being pushed through the marketplace gates and into the surrounding streets. A woman carrying a baby in a wrap around her chest turned to look at them, and said with sparkling eyes, "What an exciting day it is - Lady Fatima al Mayriti is here in town, at the Great Library!" She gave a smile so broad that you could see every single one of her teeth.

6

Fatima of Madrid

At Cordoba's main library, Lady Fatima al Mayriti was being welcomed with a great ceremony.

Iman explained in whispers to the other girls, reading quickly from the Book of Knowledge:

"Fatima al Mayriti was an Astronomer who lived in the tenth and eleventh century. She was the student of her Father, great Andalusian astronomer Maslama al-Mayriti. Seeing her intelligence and interest in the sciences and mathematics, he took care to assist and start her on her academic path, giving her the highest quality attention and education he could. Eventually, she became his partner in scientific research. Together, they worked on astronomical and mathematical experimentation and investigations of all kinds.

Through their findings, they were able to edit and make corrections to "The Astronomical Tables of al-Khwarizmi," a classical textbook of the time. They also wrote a book that explored the functions of astrolabes. Fatima developed calendars, compiled tables for trigonometric ratios and spherical trigonometry, astrological tables, Parallax tables, lunar phases and eclipses and calculated tables of the true position of the Sun, Moon and Planets.

"Amazing, she was a real math whiz!" breathed Iman.

Fatima wrote a series of books called, "Fatima Corrections."

Fatima is known to be the first woman astronomer in Andalusia, Spain – that means the first woman astronomer in the western world!"

"Wow," said Jaide. "We're going to see a celebrity!"

A man dressed in fancy, flowing robes stood on a podium. "I, Prince Hakam III, would like to officially announce that Scholar Fatima al Mayriti has been recognized as one of the greatest scholars of Andalusia!"

The crowd cheered.

The Prince handed Scholar Fatima a long robe and a hat with a flat square top. Court servants came forth to assist Fatima put them on.

"Hey!" said Jaide. "She looks like she's graduating!"

"Yes," said Iman. "This was the traditional garb of officially-recognized scholars in the Muslim world. It is from this tradition that people all over the world took the practice of dressing their graduating students in robes and hats."

"It is with great honor that I offer you, Scholar Fatima al Mayriti, an appointment as court astronomer, and member of our government. For this, you will have a court salary to continue your research, here in Córdoba!"

The crowd cheered again. The Scholar Fatima looked down in humility.

The Prince spoke again, "You are all invited to a grand banquet in honor of our Head Astronomer, where she will be our guest of honor!"

"*Now* I know where they got the idea of award ceremonies and banquets from!" said Sara.

The crowd started moving towards the palace. The Jannah Jewels stood in their places, not sure whether to join in or not, until people pushing past them turned to them and encouraged them to come along, "Come, why are you just standing there? Come on, we are all invited! Don't be shy."

Jaide grabbed the arms of her friends: "Did you catch that girls? A banquet – put on by a prince, no less!" Her eyes looked like they were watering as much as her mouth. In spite of her concerns over their mission, Hidayah had to laugh.

The Jannah Jewels joined the crowds and entered the palace. The palace's high ceilings were decorated with painted designs of flowers and vines in soft pinks and greens. The pillars were made of red and white marble. The smell of musky perfume burning in the corners of the room hung in the air.

Soon, they were seated in a great banquet hall. Jaide was overjoyed. The table was set with fancy bowls, plates, and sparkling knives and forks.

Servants ladled soup out of massive tureens into the bowls of the guests. Jaide sniffed the fragrant steaminess of the soup appreciatively, her eyes closed. She opened them, "What can I say?" and she began to eat.

After soup, succulent lamb was placed before the guests, along with a sauce of almonds and prunes. Trays of warm, crusty bread were refilled every few minutes. Side dishes of potatoes, spinach, and beans were brought out. Some of the flavors seemed the same as what the Jannah Jewels remembered from a beautiful meal they had been served ages ago, in the home of Abbas ibn Firnas.

Hidayah took in her surroundings. The atmosphere in the great hall was filled with cheer. Men and women of all kinds – from beggars to rich merchants – sat together sharing the meal. Children played about between the tables and music could be heard from musicians who sat near the royal party up at the front of the hall.

But where was Scholar Fatima? wondered Hidayah. *Shouldn't she be up there with the Prince? Or somewhere in this hall?*

As if reading Hidayah's thoughts, Jaide said: "Scholar Fatima is pretty lucky to have all this amazing food served in her honor. I bet she has the best seat in the house!"

Hidayah tried sitting up taller to scan the great hall. Hidayah scrutinized the Prince's table, filled with his ministers and close servants. But, there was no sign of the very person in whose honor they were all present.

Jaide looked up at Hidayah: "Eat up, Hidayah, you need to get some fuel in you for what lies ahead. Come on," Sara said gently, and spooned some sauce into Hidayah's plate.

But try as she might, Hidayah couldn't concentrate on her plate or her hungry stomach. She felt she must see Scholar Fatima. Somehow, she felt that there was a reason why they had been brought to this banquet, and it wasn't just to eat.

Hidayah stood up and said, "Girls, I want you to stay here. I need to go check something out. I'll be back, inshaAllah, in no more than ten minutes."

The Jannah Jewels nodded in acceptance, and hoped that whatever Hidayah was up to, she would be okay.

7

Giving Thanks

Outside in the courtyard, Hidayah gulped in the fresh air. The scent of various perfumes and tastes of rich foods had made Hidayah feel distracted from her purpose.

Hidayah inhaled and held her breath for a good five seconds, feeling the air well up in her chest, before exhaling completely out for another five seconds. She had to calm herself from the feeling of excitement that was rising inside her...it was a feeling that something very important was about to happen. *I feel like the very thing I've been looking for is about to come to me,* thought Hidayah.

In the silence of the courtyard, Hidayah slowly turned around, and there was Scholar Fatima, riding towards her on a white steed.

Scholar Fatima stopped the horse when she reached Hidayah, and smiled down at Hidayah; in her eyes was a look that made Hidayah feel like they had known each other for a long time.

"And how are you, young friend? Is everything going well?" asked Scholar Fatima.

Hidayah responded shyly, "I don't know, Scholar Fatima...."

Scholar Fatima smiled. Gently she said, "Not everything going according to plan?"

Hidayah looked down and shook her head.

Scholar Fatima was still smiling when she looked up again. "Rely on Him, Hidayah."

Tears started to fill Hidayah's eyes. She knew this was the message she needed to hear, and exactly what Sensei would say to her.

Scholar Fatima spoke again, "I must leave now, my dear. Is there anything you want to ask me before I go?"

"Yes," said Hidayah. "Why are you leaving, Scholar Fatima? Weren't you offered the highest post of all scholars, here at the royal court?"

"Yes I was. But I could never accept that, my friend."

"But why?" asked Hidayah.

"My Father is in Madrid. He is too old now to travel to move to Córdoba. He is the one who taught me all I know, and I could never leave his side. My place is there, with him. I want to serve him until the end of his days."

"But," stammered Hidayah, "but isn't it important to serve your people as well? They want you...to be their top scholar."

"Hidayah, I can serve them from Madrid. I can serve them by doing exactly what I've been doing all this time, without the fancy title, without the fame, without the salary."

"My Father is not only my Parent, he is also my Teacher. I would be so ungrateful should I walk far from him, to take the honors of this world while my true honor is in serving him, in thanks for all he has taught me," Scholar Fatima said.

Hidayah was amazed. She thought about Sensei, and all that Sensei had taught her, and wondered if she felt the same gratitude.

As if answering Hidayah's next thought, Scholar Fatima continued, "I am grateful for the appreciation the Prince has shown me, as well as all the people of this good city. But don't worry too much about them Hidayah, look," and Scholar Fatima gestured towards the great banquet hall. "They haven't even missed me. They will still be able to benefit from any knowledge that comes out of my work. But they don't need me by their side. My Father deserves that more."

Hidayah stood, riveted. Each word seemed like it was a pearl sparkling in the sunlight. She looked up at Scholar Fatima with a new kind of admiration. More than just a math and science whiz,

Scholar Fatima had a special wisdom that Hidayah recognized.

"Now, I have a word of advice for you, Hidayah: Do the right thing by thanking those who have brought you to where you are. If you do that, you will be shown how to go forth in the right way..."

Hidayah slowly nodded.

Then something occurred to her: "But Scholar Fatima, why did you come all this way if you didn't want to accept this position?"

"It's good manners to accept an invitation, isn't it? Besides, I had a little something I had to get done here." She smiled a knowing smile. It seemed to Hidayah like her eyes gave a wink. "God be with you, Hidayah," she said, and before Hidayah could respond, she was gone.

Hidayah stood stock still. Scholar Fatima's words echoed in her heart and mind. Then she realized something incredible: Scholar Fatima had known her name. She had called her "Hidayah."

In the silence of the courtyard, Hidayah heard a faint tinkling sound at her feet. She looked down.

Rolling in the dust on its side, was a small, glass vial...

What?! Oh my God. It couldn't be! Was it?

At first, Hidayah just stood, staring. Then, as if in slow motion, she bent down and picked up the vial. As she dusted it off, she saw the colour of what was inside.

★   ★   ★   ★   ★

Back in the hall, the guests were now being served dessert. Plates of steamed pears in tarragon sauce and light lemon custards decorated with mint leaves were being passed around. Jaide had accepted both plates at once, and was now alternating between them, a bite from here, a bite from there. She had a look of sheer joy on her face.

When Hidayah took her place at the table next to Iman, Iman could see something special had happened to Hidayah. Wiping her mouth, very lady-like with the folded napkin that had been on her lap, she gave Hidayah a quizzical look.

Hidayah held up the bottle. "From Scholar Fatima."

8

The Scientific Method

"What?" gasped Sara. "Is it the artifact??"

In answer, Hidayah stood up from the table, and the Jannah Jewels followed suit. The four girls slipped out of the banquet hall and into a corridor of the palace where they could talk without fear of being overheard.

Hidayah showed the others the bottle and they stared at it closely.

"It's a red powder!"

"But the stopper is not the same stopper as the one we are looking for!" exclaimed Jaide, having forgotten her dessert altogether.

"Wait," Iman took the vial of crimson, that was from Yeshua, out of her pocket and held it up next to the one from Scholar Fatima. "I think we might be able to switch the stoppers – they seem the same size!"

Gently, Sara removed each lid, and then she placed the lid from Yeshua on the bottle from Scholar Fatima.

Amazingly, wonderfully, it fit perfectly!

"Alhamdulillah!"

Iman opened up the *Book of Knowledge*. "This artifact, it's got something to do with Scholar Fatima, that's for sure."

Iman read out loud:

Maslama al Mayriti worked extensively in the science of alchemy, and discovered various methods for the purification of precious metals. Maslama was the first to mention the principle of the conservation of mass, which he discovered in a groundbreaking experiment on mercuric oxide.

He wrote:

I took natural, quivering mercury, free from impurity, and placed it in a glass vessel shaped like an egg. This,

51

I put inside another vessel like a cooking pot, and set the whole apparatus over an extremely gentle fire. The outer pot was then in such a degree of heat that I could barely put my hand upon it. I heated the apparatus, day and night for forty days, after which I opened it. I found that the mercury (the original weight of which was a quarter of a pound) had been completely converted into red powder, soft to touch, but the weight remaining as it was originally.

"Red powder, soft to touch..." echoed Sara, staring intently at the vial. "Well, this is what we have here."

Jaide spoke up: "All that is left now, is to get the second bottle."

"Girls," spoke up Hidayah. "Before we move on so quickly, I need to tell you a message Scholar Fatima gave me. She said: *Do the right thing by thanking those who have brought you to where you are. If you do so, you will be shown how to go forth in the right way...*"

"That sounds like something Sensei would say," remarked Jaide.

Then, suddenly, words of her Sensei came into Hidayah's mind too, *It's not about hitting your target, it's about your heart.*

"Jannah Jewels... I feel like this is the key. We've been so focused in every mission on hitting our target - finding the artifact and making it home. But, we haven't really done things the right way. I mean, we're always in a rush to get to the end, and we forget about the 'how.' There are so many people who help us along the way each time. And have we really thanked them?"

"We always say thank you to everyone who helps us! Don't we?" said Jaide.

"Yes, we say it with our mouths, that's easy. Maybe we do that out of habit, just to be polite. But what about our actions and hearts? Is there thankfulness there?" said Hidayah. "Girls, listen. The reason Scholar Fatima didn't stay is because she wants to show her thankfulness to her Father, her Teacher. She left all this glory to be with him."

"Wow. That is amazing."

"Sometimes we barely even think about the people, the friends, the teachers even, after we benefit from their help - until the next time we need help from them."

Sara cleared her throat and spoke up clearly, "That's what I was trying to tell you – reminding you how Abbas asked us to pray about his flight. But you were all so busy."

"And now it's too late! Now it's already hundreds of years later. We never prayed for him. I remember, we all said, Yes! Definitely! Yet, when the time passed, we forgot. Maybe he flew from the wrong place, maybe he got hurt!" cried Jaide.

Hidayah said, "Look, it's never too late. This is what God tells us. Let us make a prayer now. At least, let's be true to our promise, even if it's later than it should be."

The girls held up their hands and silently prayed for all those who had helped them on this mission. They prayed for Abbas, they prayed for Yeshua, and they prayed for Scholar Fatima.

Finally, Hidayah started to feel they were on the right track again. It felt so good to try to *do the right thing*.

"I only wish we could have gone back to politely and sincerely thank Abbas and Yeshua in person," said Jaide.

"I wonder if that's the only way we'll finish this mission," said Sara quietly.

9

More Messages

After wandering the palace hallways for a few hours, the girls now found themselves inside a vast library. It was the royal library.

"Golly, Glory to God! This is awesome! The Royal Library of Córdoba!" exclaimed Iman.

There were huge ceilings and all along the walls were bookshelves that seemed to reach up several storeys high.

There was a smell of fine aloeswood burning, adding a sacredness to the space. Several individuals, in robes and turbans, stood holding books or searching for a title; others sat at long, wooden tables with several volumes spread before them.

At a wooden desk in the middle of the library, sat a woman in green robes. She was patiently writing with a quill pen upon a huge scroll of paper. Two women close to the Jannah Jewels stood silently admiring her work. The girls overheard the women say the name, "Lubna."

Iman quickly flipped through the Book of Knowledge. She pulled the Jewels to a corner of the library and read:

"This is Lubna of Córdoba. She was raised in the palace of the Sultan Abd al Rahman III and despite humble beginnings, she quickly became one of the most important figures in the Andalusian Palace at the time. She became the Prince's secretary and scribe as well as a secretary to his son, Hakam II Ibn Abd al Rahman. Lubna was quite an extraordinary figure; one of her roles was presiding over the royal library. The library, which at the time included 500 thousand books, was one of the most important libraries in the world.'"

"MashaAllah! How fascinating! Is there more? Keep reading!" exclaimed Jaide.

"Yes there is! Listen..." whispered Iman.

"*Lubna's love and knowledge of math was great and as if that was not enough, she was also a philosopher, a poet, and a calligrapher who left behind 'beautiful works of calligraphy.' The historian Ibn Bashkvl said, "She mastered the writing and science of poetry, and her knowledge of mathematics was broad and great. She has also mastered many other sciences and there was no one nobler then her in the Ummayad Palace.*"

"*It is told that while walking in the roads of Andalusia she would teach children the principles of math and the multiplication tables. This was her form of showing thankfulness for all she had been taught.*"

Hidayah let out a deep breath. "Girls, girls, look how she gave back – gave to others, in *gratitude*."

Suddenly, a murmur spread across the library. A petite woman had just entered the library. She went directly to Lubna and the two embraced warmly.

All eyes were glued on them, and the Jewels heard whispers:

"It's Poet Aisha bint Ahmad bin Muhammad!" said a woman in a crisp white hijab.

"Her poems are just magnificent!" said a young girl, clambering to stand up.

"Did you read the last one?" asked her friend equally joyful at the sight of Poet Aisha.

Iman quickly flipped back to another page in the Book of Knowledge.

"This is Aisha bint Ahmad bin Muhammad from Córdoba. She was a poet and a writer whose calligraphy was so beautiful she was commissioned to do the printing of several copies of the Holy Book. She was a rich woman who spent her fortune on her huge collection of books and for charity. The historian, Ibn Hayyan, said of her: 'There was no one in Andalusia at her time who was as learned and intelligent and eloquent as she.'"

"Wow, what amazing women! " said Jaide.

"I want to go up and meet them," said Iman. "Come on, this is our chance. You got to meet Scholar Fatima, now let's meet Poet Aisha and Scholar Lubna!"

Iman pulled the Jewels forward.

As they reached the two women, Iman stuttered, "Uhm... as-salaamu' alaykum."

"Wa-alaikum as-salaam Wa Rahmatullah, dear girls." The scholars replied, reaching out their hands.

"We're the Jannah Jewels and we are on a mission to retrieve a missing artifact. We have travelled back in time. We failed our last mission and are determined to succeed, with the Help from God," said Iman.

Poet Aisha took a long look at Iman. Iman straightened her shirt, pushed her eye-glasses back on her nose that were slipping off from the sweat drops forming all over Iman's face.

Iman felt she had to speak again, "You are women of such great learning! I would love to be like you." She could not contain her excitement. Iman's favourite past-time was writing poems about God's creation.

Poet Aisha spoke softly, "Iman, you are intelligent, and you love learning. But these are not enough. Information like you have in this book can help, but you must gain true knowledge. True knowledge comes from people. And you must gain wisdom. Wisdom comes from the Most High to those who are humble."

Poet Aisha continued, "Iman, you must stop relying on just your Book of Knowledge there in your hand and let yourself learn from the people God puts in your life."

"And with that, you must learn to honor the elders, those who know more than you," said Scholar Lubna.

Mathematician Lubna stood and rolled up the scroll she had been writing on, which had dried by now.

"Here, daughters, take this: it will serve as a gentle reminder of the lesson you have valiantly learned today."

Again, Iman slid her glasses back onto her nose. She cleared her throat and read the first verse of *Ayatul Kursi, the verse of the Throne.*

Poet Aisha looked approvingly at Iman. Then, she looked at Sara. "Sara, the time has come for your tool."

Sara was shocked! "My tool! Yes!" She quickly opened her backpack and took out the metal ball, handing it respectfully to Poet Aisha.

The Jannah Jewels looked on as Poet Aisha pressed a few of the embedded markings on the ball. The markings on the ball were ancient hieroglyphics and Scholar Lubna silently directed Poet Aisha which order to press them in. They worked together in harmony and sisterhood.

Click!

The Jannah Jewels gasped!

A small latch opened on the ancient metal ball, revealing a secret compartment underneath it. Poet Aisha handed it back to Sara.

Finally! How would I have ever figured that out! What a blessing from God to meet these wise women! thought Sara.

When Sara looked at the tiny secret compartment inside the metal ball, she couldn't believe what she saw, but she understood exactly what to do with it.

It was a smaller version of the Golden Clock!

"How can we ever thank you?" Sara looked up shyly at Poet Aisha and Scholar Lubna.

They smiled back at her gently. "I think you've just thanked us, dear," said Aisha.

Lubna added, "Sometimes, the only way you can thank someone is to remember them in your prayers, when no one but God is looking and listening. That's proof you really are grateful."

10

Back in Time

Hidayah and Iman hopped onto Spirit, Iman's horse, and Jaide and Sara jumped onto Jaide's skateboard. They raced through the market with swiftness and ease.

"It's so amazing, the ancient metal ball, Sara!" said Jaide.

"Yes, all we have to do is turn the clock back in my ancient metal ball and it will take us right back to the time of Abbas ibn Firnas – his spot is 4 o'clock on the Golden Clock," exclaimed Sara.

"When your miniature Golden Clock takes us back, I have a feeling my time-travel watch is going to be unstuck from the 1 o'clock position it's been in all this time," said Jaide.

The Jannah Jewels finally reached the outskirts of Córdoba. There in the distance, they could see a tree. Finally reaching it, they disembarked and pushed with all their might against its trunk.

Down, down, down they tumbled, landing with a thud in the bottom of the tree. The Jewels stood silently and all, except for Sara, held hands. Sara stood in the middle, pressing with her finger on the position of 4 o'clock in her ancient metal ball.

Closing their eyes, the Jewels calmly intoned, *"Bismillahir-Rahmanir-Rahim."*

"Allahu Akbar!" a few moments later, the Jannah Jewels opened their eyes. Alhamdulillah! It worked! They were back in the Ancient Spain they had first arrived in!

"We're here on the right side of town; let's go see if Yeshua's here," suggested Iman.

"Yes," said Sara, "we still need that other bottle, let's not forget, in order to complete the mission. I just hope it's not too late – Yeshua was about to travel..."

"Girls, what are you saying? Didn't you learn the lesson? This is not about the artifact, anymore. We need to do the right thing if we ever hope to get home. Now, it's time to find Abbas ibn Firnas and express our sincere heartfelt thanks for the advice he gave us and his kindness to us, and make sure he is okay after his flight!" said Hidayah.

Iman spoke quietly, "I'm sorry it came out wrong. That's what I meant. When you talked about being grateful, well, Yeshua is also someone we owe gratefulness too, that's all I meant. I think we should actually return his vial to him, the crimson one."

Hidayah looked intently at Iman, and then nodded with a smile. "Yes Iman, you are right. Thank you."

The Jannah Jewels made their way into the city precincts. They were so relieved to arrive at the square, and see that it was just as it used to be – the Archery Supply Shop and Yeshua's Pharmacy just the way they had been when they had seen them the first time.

The Jannah Jewels stumbled toward Yeshua ben Yousef's store, quite tired by now. Would Yeshua still be there?

"As-salaamu' alaykum!" said the Jannah Jewels in unison.

"Hello my friends! It's you again! What brings you here? Do you need another bottle?" asked Yeshua.

The girls were embarrassed. They realized how much they took, took, took. Now was the time to give back. Hidayah spoke up: "No, we really are just here to thank you, Sir. And we want to return this to you." Iman pulled the crimson out of her pocket, "Sorry, it's not the same lid, is that okay?"

"Oh yes, this lid is nicer," said Yeshua, looking at the pearl inlaid stopper. I've never seen this style before – super modern looking! Thank you girls, that was really considerate of you."

"We thought we might not find you here – what about your trip to the Holy Land?" said Hidayah.

"Oh no dear, I actually missed my caravan that day. Maybe you forgot to pray for this old man," he said with a smile.

The girls looked down. Maybe Yeshua was joking, but his words made them worry again about Abbas ibn Firnas.

"We have something special to say, Yeshua."

The girls smiled as Hidayah offered thanks in a way she knew would be pleasing to Yeshua's heart.

"Your great grandchildren will carry on your business well into the future, Sir. They will continue to develop this wonderful trade you have and you would be proud if you could see them!"

"God is Great, praise be to Him for granting me such a beautiful vision. Thank you, Jannah Jewels for bringing me such good news," said Yeshua.

"Now, we need to go, Sir. We need to find Sir Abbas ibn Firnas! We'll come back after we see him. We might need to get another bottle from you, but first things first!"

"Girls, I wish I had something special like ambergris to give you; if you come across it, keep it. Don't bring it back to me, it's yours!"

11

Blinded

Just as the Jewels were leaving the square, who should they bump into, but Jasmin!

Jasmin's eyebrows were furrowed. Her grey dress circled around her as she stopped and planted her feet in position.

Hidayah reached for her bow and arrow and took up her stance.

"Not this time, Jasmin," she said.

Hidayah steadied her bow and thought back to her Sensei at the top of the hill at the dojo when she was asked for the first time after months of practice to shoot her first arrow. It was a special time because it was the same day that the Sensei had taught Hidayah a special practice that helped Hidayah in her form. Hidayah bent her head down and focused on the beat of her heart. She looked down for a brief moment; her bow was in a perfect circle as the arrow sat effortlessly in a straight line, perpendicular to the bow and parallel to the ground.

But, Jasmin did not take up a stance. She simply walked forward, right up to the Jewels. Hidayah slowly lowered her bow.

Jasmin reached out her hand. In it, was the vial of ambergris. "I thought I should give this back to you." The girls were delighted to see the bottle – the very thing they needed. They knew Jasmin still thought it was the wrong artifact.

Hidayah looked hard at Jasmin. Was it really generosity on her part when she was under the impression that ambergris was not the right artifact? What did it matter, though. Hidayah reached out to take the bottle. Jasmin looked at Hidayah curiously and then she opened up the bottle and the ambergris created dust all around them.

"Cover your eyes!" screamed Jaide.

Hidayah pushed Jasmin aside with renewed vigor, seeing through the ambergris dust with her intense eyes. That's what Hidayah was known for! Her sight!

The Jewels started to run through the marketplace, running to the home of Abbas ibn Firnas. For a brief moment, Hidayah looked back. There was Jasmin, still hunched over on the ground, coughing.

The Jannah Jewels looked at each other, panting from all the running. Finally, Jaide spoke up, "Girls, look, we've got the two artifacts, we've thanked Yeshua, and now....maybe we should just head home. We don't want to get caught by Jaffar after all this. And I know what you are thinking, but believe me, Abbas would not mind. Abbas would tell us to *do the right thing.*"

"And the right thing, Jaide," said Hidayah in a stern voice, "is going to thank Abbas in person. We've had enough adventure to teach us that lesson, I would think! Come on! Now!"

"How could I be so naïve," thought Hidayah. *"I have to be so careful around that Jasmin."*

Suddenly, out of a corner, Jaffar jumped out and into the path of the Jewels. This time thankfully, he was without Moe and Slim. Jaide, Sara and Hidayah managed to dodge him, but Jaffar tripped Iman, pulling her down. She fell, but successfully wiggled out of his reach. The only problem was, her glasses had been thrown from her face as she fell, and now lay a few feet away from her, broken.

12

Sight

Hidayah ran back and picked Iman up off the floor. Jaide was already getting on her skateboard, and quickly pulled her friends onto it.

Jaffar was yellng after them, "Give me the bottle - I know you have it!"

With a whoosh, Jaide pulled the skateboard up a hill so fast that it took off a few feet into the air. The girls held on tight, soaring in the air. Abbas would have been impressed.

They raced forward until finally landing in front of Abbas ibn Firnas's home. The girls felt such relief that they started to cry.

This was the moment of truth. If Abbas had flown from the wrong place, there might be no one able to answer the door!

Hidayah closed her eyes and said another prayer. Gently, Jaide knocked on the door.

There was no answer.

Iman knocked. Again, no answer.

Finally, Sara knocked. She prayed and prayed as she knocked.

But, no answer.

Hidayah felt like she had truly failed. Everything seemed to go black around her as sadness overwhelmed her. Iman tugged at her sleeve – "Hidayah, have hope."

Suddenly, a voice called out from behind them, "As-salaamu' alaykum!"

It was Abbas ibn Firnas! And he was walking, healthy!

"My dear daughters, how are you?" he said.

They ran to him. Jaide jumped up and down out of joy.

"You're alive!" said Sara with tears in her eyes.

"Thanks be to God, yes, I am, my dear children," said Abbas.

"How was your flying, sir?" asked Jaide.

Abbas smiled a huge smile. "Thanks be to God, and thank you for your prayers for me!"

The girls looked at one another joyfully.

"I'm sure it made all the difference. Now come on inside. Wait a minute. There is something different about you, Iman. Oh yes, where are your glasses? Are you okay?" asked Abbas ibn Firnas.

"They broke! She can't see well without them," said Hidayah.

"Oh, no problem! I happen to have the equipment to make a new pair! Come right in," said Abbas.

When Abbas had made new lenses and set them in a wire frame for Iman, the first thing Iman saw was a bottle. A bottle just like the ones in Yeshua's store.

"What's this?" asked Iman.

"This is the sand I used to make your new lens," said Abbas.

Iman gasped. "How can I ever thank you? You taught me a lot, sir, and even then, I jumped to a lot of conclusions."

"I want to thank you, and always remember your kindness to us. Ohhh! Wait!! I get it! I think I finally get it! I think I found the second artifact!" exclaimed Iman.

"Really?" asked Sara. She was so excited, she could hardly stay still.

"Yes! It's this bottle. I get it now. It's *special*," said Iman.

"So, you think you came all this way just to collect a bottle of something as simple as sand?" asked Abbas ibn Firnas; he smiled a knowing smile.

Iman remembered her words: It was as if she was going back in time, and being shown where she made a wrong turn.

> "It's got to be one of these…exotic items…I just don't think we'd be sent all the way here to find a bottle of…well, sand or salt! You know?"

"Unless, said Abbas, speaking very slowly. "Unless that salt had a specific significance to the place or time or persons…and then it would fit one of your three conditions for being an artifact…"

"It's special to me," she said to Abbas. "It's special to me because it is a symbol of your kindness to us, Sir. We came back to thank you. I think we can never really thank you enough for what you have done for us, but we want you to know how much we appreciate it, truly."

"Pray for me, daughter," said Abbas ibn Firnas.

"This time, right away, instead of just saying yes!" said Hidayah.

Iman bent her head and actually made a sincere du'a right then for Abbas ibn Firnas.

13

Click

The Jannah Jewels finally reached the tree and pushed against the trunk with all their might. They heard the familiar click as the door of the trunk opened. They jumped onto the slide and whooshed down, down, down, landing with a thump. They held hands and said, "*Bismillahir-Rahmanir-Rahim.*" When they opened their eyes, they were at the bottom of a familiar tree in a familiar time.

As the Jannah Jewels all sat down in a heap on the ground, the Sensei appeared from out of the dark shadows with a look of concern mixed with relief on her face. Then, the three other Masters appeared next to Sensei. They all walked over to the Golden Clock. Nervously, Hidayah kneeled and took the two vials out of her cargo pockets: ambergris from

Jasmin and the vial from Scholar Fatima, mercury. She reached over and handed them to Iman.

Iman took one vial out of her pocket as well: sand. She examined the three vials in her hand: ambergris, mercury and sand. She put the ambergris down. There was barely any left in the vial after Jasmin threw it up in the air. She took the mercury and placed it at 4 o'clock. Then, she took sand and placed it at 5 o'clock. All of a sudden, the entire tree shone with a bright light as the two vials "clicked" into place.

"Alhamdulillahi Rabbil al Ameen!" they all exclaimed.

"You've learned a lot of valuable lessons in this mission," said Sensei with a broad smile. "It's not easy to learn the virtue of thankfulness. Sometimes, you have to be really "stuck" to learn it."

"Stuck as in super stuck, like back in time!" said Jaide. "There was a point when I thought we would never come back."

Master Horseback Rider approached Iman and whispered words of encouragement. Iman nodded in humility at her words.

"I will take my time to "see" things for what they are and not jump to conclusions," said Iman pushing the glasses Abbas ibn Firnas fixed back on her nose. "I will respect how the most simple things like salt and sand hold so much weight in this world. Simple people and simple things should not be overlooked."

"Dear Jannah Jewels, you are almost halfway through your mission to save the world," said Sensei. You have gained strength from your weaknesses and you have grown in the shelter of one another in a beautiful way. But, there is more work and more challenges that await you. I am certain that you have what it takes."

With that, the Masters turned and left with their flowing robes disappearing around the corner of the library, in the bottom of the tree.

"Let's go home, Jewels!" exclaimed Jaide.

They climbed out of the tree into the cool night. Hidayah and Iman wrapped their arms around each other's waists. Sara and Jaide ran in front, adding cartwheels out of joy in the neighbourhood park that the maple time-travel tree was in.

The sun was setting and Hidayah observed the shades of purple and pink the sun made in the sky. She looked thoughtful. She slid her strands of hair into her scarf and walked a little taller. She had a familiar bounce back in her step.

"Hey, Jewels, let's go pray Maghrib, the sunset prayer, in the masjid together and thank God for returning us home safely," said Hidayah.

"Great idea!" The girls responded and walked briskly to their local masjid a few blocks away.

After the prayer, Hidayah's thoughts turned for a moment to Jaffar and Jasmin while she was making her dua's, her supplications. She decided right then and there to include both Jaffar and Jasmin in her supplications. There was something tugging at her heart about them – she couldn't quite figure out the strange sadness Jaffar and Jasmin had in their steel, iron-grey eyes. She finished her prayers and smiled at her friends who smiled back. They looked peaceful and relaxed sitting all in a row, united in faith and friendship.

"Will Hidayah have the strength to find the remaining 7 artifacts? Will Jasmin and Jaffar work together to beat Hidayah and the Jannah Jewels? Will Khan be furious with his son? Find out in Jannah Jewels Book 6: Mystery in Morocco.

Don't miss the next Jannah Jewels book!

Solving riddles, finding clues and surprising twists await you in Book 6 of the Jannah Jewels Adventure Series. Will the Jannah Jewels solve the riddles and get back in time?

Or will they be stuck in time again? Find the answers in the next book as the Jewels travel to Mysterious Morocco!

Find out more about the sixth book by visiting our website:

www.JannahJewels.com

Glossary

Alhamdulillahi Rabbil Al-Ameen: "All praise is due to God" in Arabic. This prayer is said when thankful of something or to show appreciation.

Allah: God

As-salaamu' alaykum: "May the peace of God be with you" in Arabic.

BismillahirRahmanirRaheem: "In the name of God, Most Merciful, Most Beneficent" in Arabic. This prayer is said before partaking in something.

Hijab: a head-scarf

InshaAllah: "If it is God's will" in Arabic. It is said when indicating hope for something to occur in the future.

Jannah: heaven, paradise or garden

Mosque: A sacred place of worship for Muslims, also commonly called a masjid.

Qur'an: The last holy scripture of the Muslims.

SubhanAllah: "Glory be to God" in Arabic. This prayer is said when in awe of something.

Wa-alaikum as-salaam: "May the peace of God be upon you too" in Arabic

JANNAH JEWELS

To find out more about our other books,
go to:

www.JannahJewels.com

Made in the USA
Monee, IL
21 November 2024